George Goes to Washington

Johnny Honnold

To Mom, Dad, William, Grant, and Walter.

About 250 years ago, our founding fathers risked their lives to create a government run by the people. Democracy is a rare and fragile form of government, and it can't be taken for granted. In order for our experiment in democracy to survive, we need the younger generations to actively participate. This book is my way of getting the next generation involved.

Once upon a time, in a small town, there lived a curious young boy named George. He was an adventurous child who loved learning new things. One sunny afternoon, George's mom picked him up from school, and he noticed a bright and colorful "I Voted" sticker on her blouse.

"Mom, what's that sticker for?" George asked, pointing to the sticker on her shirt.

"Oh this?" said George's Mom, "I got it because I voted in the election today."

George had always been interested in government, and so he asked his mom, "What happens once you vote for someone? And what happens if they win the election?"

I VOTED

Washington D.C
52 Miles
52 -6

George's mom told George that when someone wins an election they go to work in Washington D.C., but she did not know what they did once they got there. So, in order to find out more about the legislative, executive, and judicial branches of the United States Government, George and his mom took a trip to Washington D.C., the capital of the United States.

Once they got there George and his mom visited the Washington Monument, the tallest structure in D.C. The monument represents the respect and gratitude our country has for George Washington, the 1st President of the United States.

Then George and his mom went to where the legislative branch works, the US Capitol Building. "What happens here?" George asked. His mom explained that Congress makes the laws of the United States, and that Congress is divided into two parts: the Senate and the House of Representatives.

Inside the Capitol, they met a senator. The politician explained that there are 2 senators that represent each state to make up a 100 person senate. They have the power to pass laws and to confirm people that want jobs like judges and ambassadors.

George and his mother then went to the other side of the Capitol to explore the House of Representatives. There, they met one of the 435 members of the House of Representatives who told George that each state gets a certain number of representatives based on how big their state's population is. Smaller states like Vermont and Delaware only have one representative but California, a big state, has 53 representatives. The Representative explained that once the House of Representatives and the Senate pass a bill, it goes to the president to sign into law.

Then George and his mom went to the White House, the home and workplace of the president. The president, as head of the executive branch, enforces and executes the laws made by Congress.

After looking at all 132 rooms and 35 bathrooms of the White House, they visited the Oval Office. This is where the president makes important decisions for the country.

After introducing himself, Mr. President explained that he is the chief of the executive branch. That means that he can veto or override the bills that congress passes, enforce the laws that congress created, and command the United States's military. The veto is something that allows the president to reject a law passed by Congress if he doesn't like it. If a bill is vetoed, it is sent back to Congress where they can try to make the bill pass again. But, now, they would need 2/3 of support from the members in Congress, not just 1/2.

VETO

Right before they left, George noticed a donkey pin on the President's chest, and he asked Mr. President why he wore it. The President explained that he and other representatives come from two main groups, which are called parties; they have different ideas about how to make our country better. He told George that his donkey pin represents his party.

So, George and his mom went to the museum to learn more about the history of parties in America. The Donkey that Mr. President was wearing represents the Democratic Party. When compared to Republicans, the other major party, Democrats generally support high taxes and more government involvement in the economy. The most prominent leaders of the democratic party in recent history are Franklin D. Roosevelt, John F. Kennedy, and Barack Obama.

History and Values
of the Democratic Party

REPUBLICAN
RUPUBLIC
REPUBLICAN PARTY
AN PARTY

Then, George and his mom went to research the Republican Party. The Republican Party, also known as the Grand Ole Party or GOP, is represented by an elephant. Individuals from this party generally support low taxes and less government involvement in the economy. The most famous leaders of the party in recent history are Ronald Reagan, George W. Bush, and Donald Trump.

George and his Mom then walked to the next exhibit where they saw a big document covered by glass. The document was labeled "the Constitution of the United States of America." Noticing that he was interested, George's Mom explained that the Constitution is a document that was written in 1787 that has the rules for how our country works. It tells us how the government is set up and what rights people have. It's like the instruction book for our country to make sure everyone is treated fairly and things run smoothly.

U.S CONSTITUTION
We the People

George's Mom then explained that there are people who make a living interpreting the Constitution. Since the document was written over 200 years ago, sometimes it is unclear what the authors meant when they wrote the Constitution. So, judges interpret the Constitution and decide whether we are still following their recipe.

To learn more about judges and the judicial branch,
George and his Mom went to the Supreme Court
of the United States.

EQUAL·JUSTICE·UNDER·LAW

In the Supreme Court, George and his Mom watched the Justices of the Supreme Court arguing about the Constitution. There are 9 Supreme Court Justices, and each one is appointed by the President and confirmed by the Senate. These Justices listen to cases and decide how the laws should be applied, protecting everyone's rights and freedoms.

Throughout history the Supreme Court has made some really important decisions about the Constitution and what it protects. In **1954**, in a case called Brown v Board of Education, the Court decided that kids of all races should be able to go to school together. In **1919**, in a case called Schenck v United States, the Court decided that free speech can be limited if it causes a big danger to others. And in **2000**, in a case called Bush v Gore, the Court decided who won a really close presidential election by stopping a recount of votes.

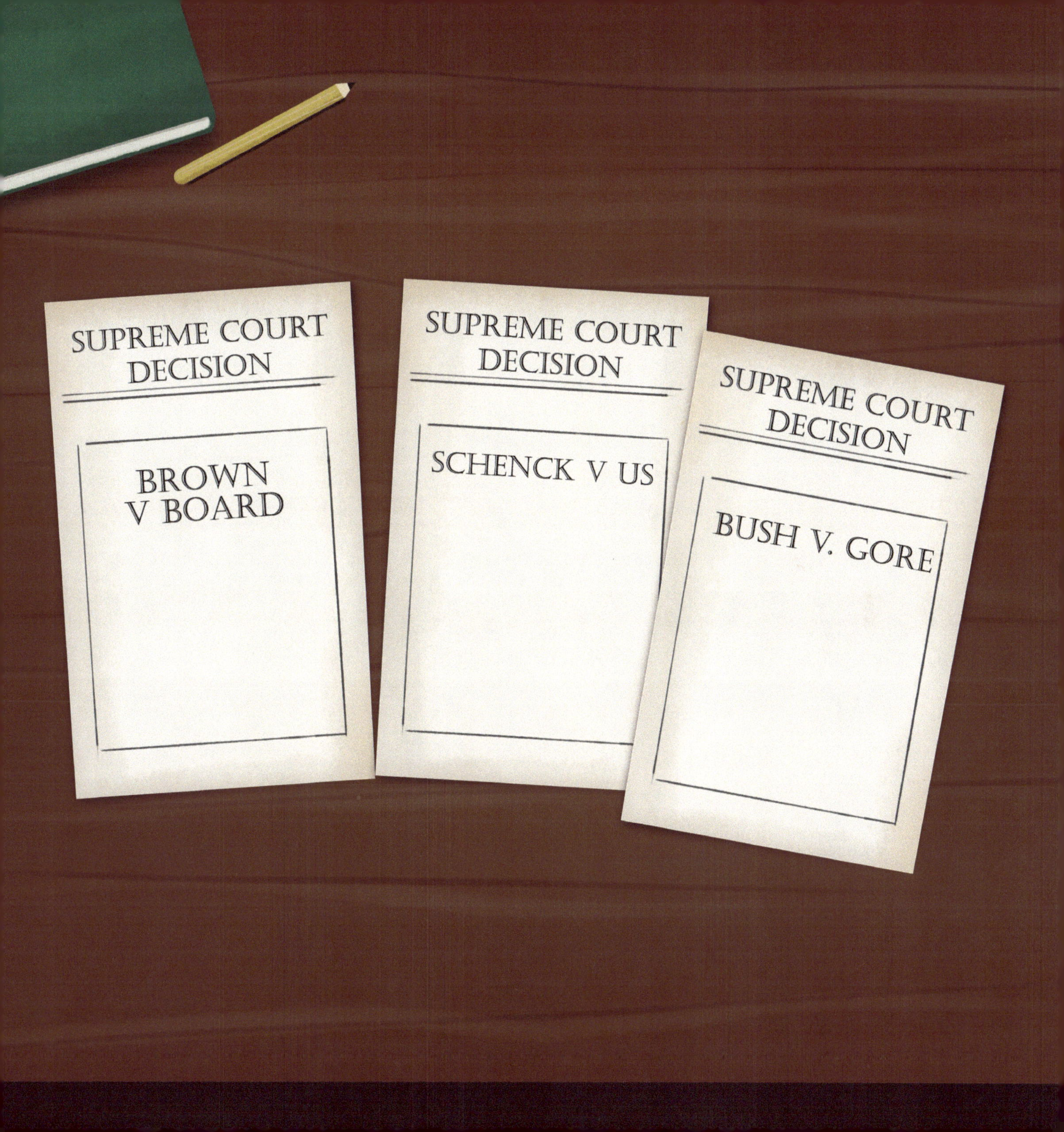

SUPREME COURT
DECISION

BROWN
V BOARD

SUPREME COURT
DECISION

SCHENCK V US

SUPREME COURT
DECISION

BUSH V. GORE

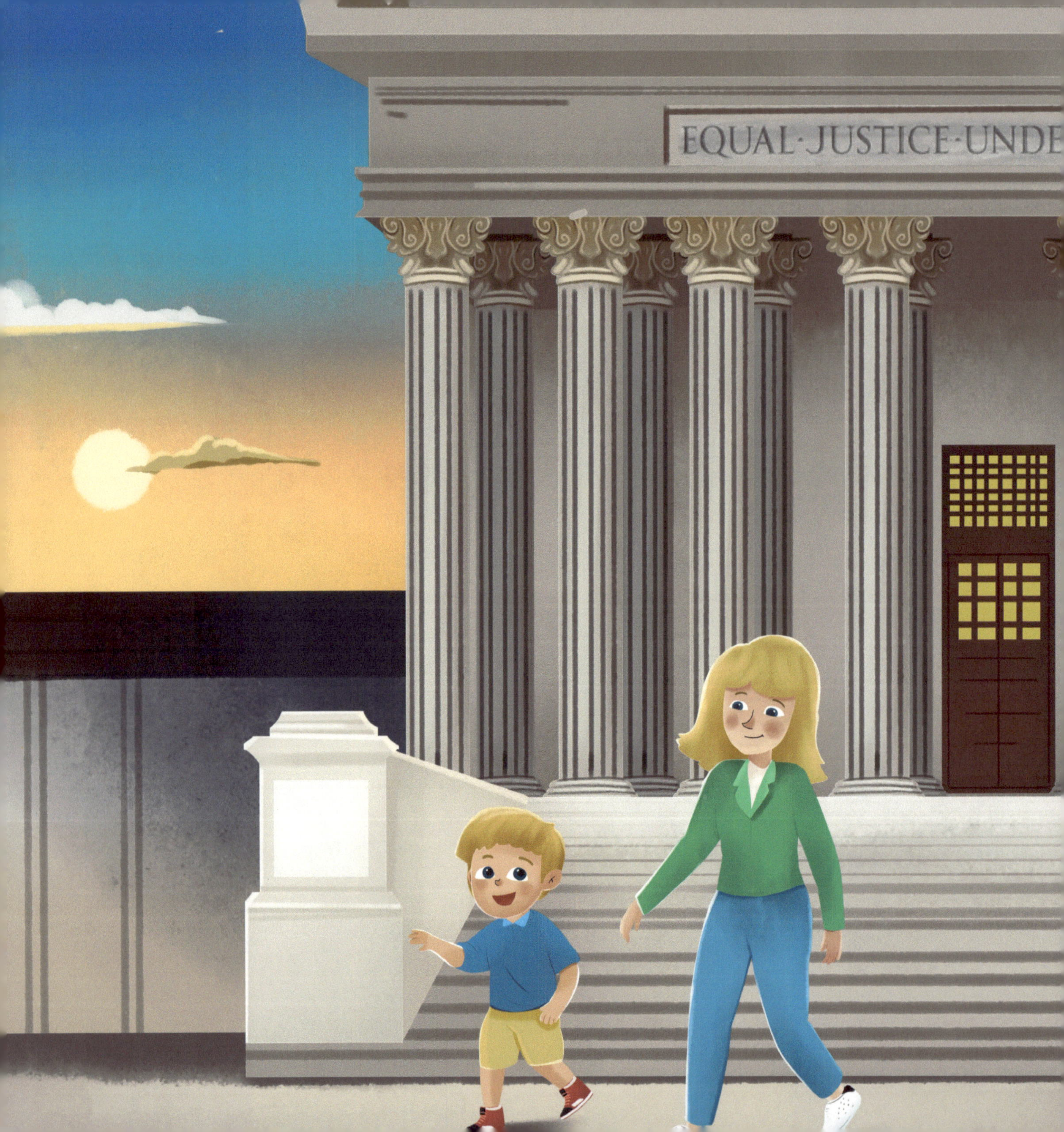

EQUAL·JUSTICE·UNDE

After Court ended for the day, George asked his mother if they could go eat dinner.

And so, George and his mom went to dinner. George got a huge burger, and, after a long day, ate the entire thing.

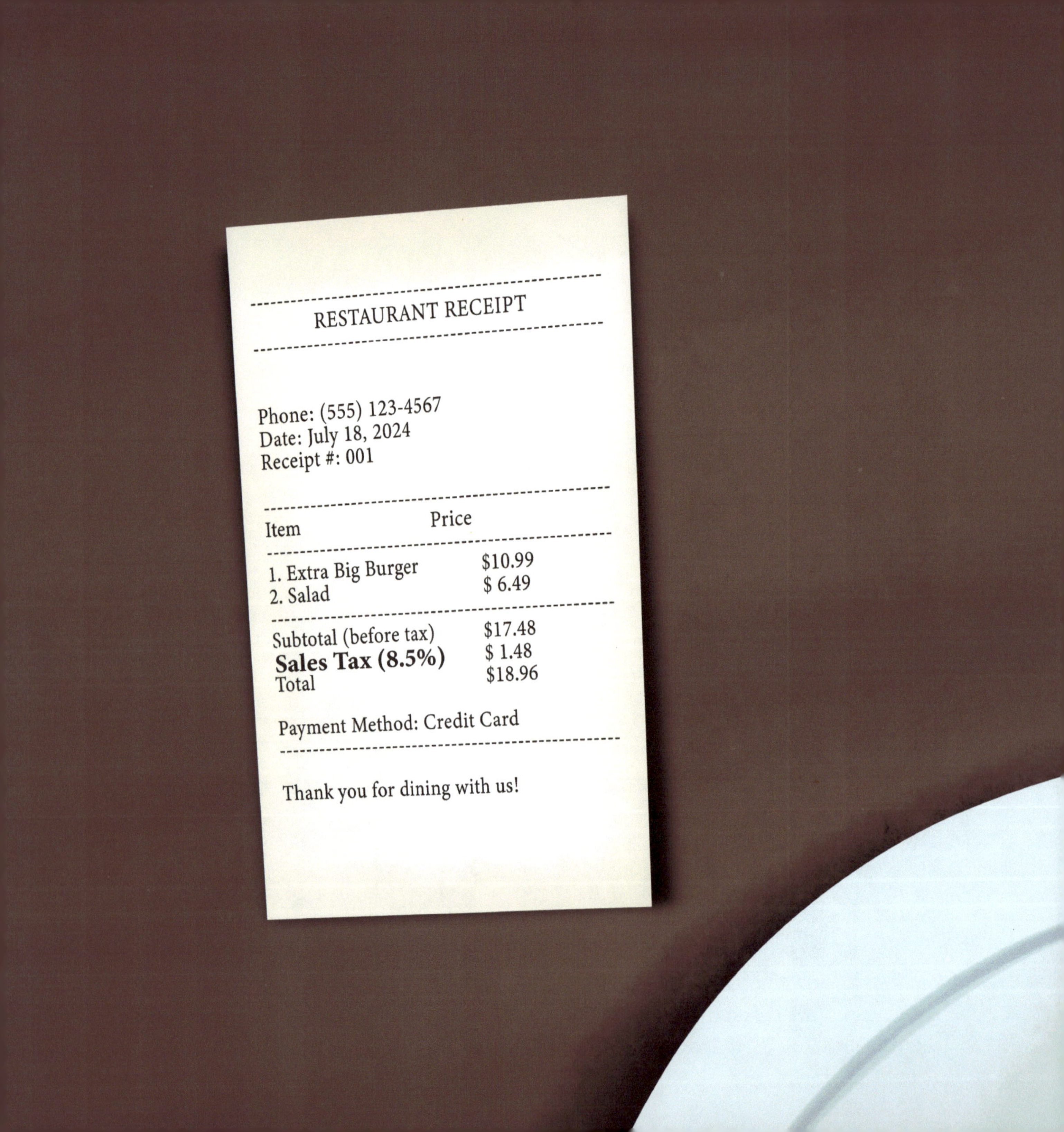

RESTAURANT RECEIPT

Phone: (555) 123-4567
Date: July 18, 2024
Receipt #: 001

Item	Price
1. Extra Big Burger	$10.99
2. Salad	$ 6.49
Subtotal (before tax)	$17.48
Sales Tax (8.5%)	$ 1.48
Total	$18.96

Payment Method: Credit Card

Thank you for dining with us!

When it was time to pay. George looked at the bill, and realized that they were getting charged for something called "tax." George's mom explained to him that taxes are imposed by the government on every purchase. She then told George that the government uses all of that money to pay for stuff like his school, the roads, and the salaries of police officers.

After they finished dinner, George and his mom got back in the car to drive home. George's mom explained to him that, eventually, he'll have to start paying taxes too. But what made George most excited was the fact that when he's 18, he'll be able to get an "I voted" sticker just like his mom.

Washington D.C
52 Miles